The Piano Recital

The Piano Recital

Richard L. Baldwin
Illustrations by Jan Kenny

*Barb,
With thanks for the joy you bring to others through music. Please enjoy.
Fondly,
Rich 2-25-00*

Buttonwood Press
Haslett, Michigan

Copyright © 1999 by Richard L. Baldwin

All rights reserved. No part of this book may be reproduced or transmitted in any form or by any means, electronic or mechanical, including photocopying, recording, or by any information storage and retrieval system, without permission in writing from the publisher.

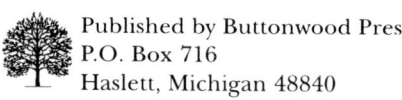
Published by Buttonwood Press
P.O. Box 716
Haslett, Michigan 48840

Publisher's Cataloging-in-Publication Data
Baldwin, Richard L.
    The piano recital / by Richard L. Baldwin. Illustrations by Jan Kenny – Haslett, MI: Buttonwood Press, 1999.
    p. ill. cm.
    ISBN 0-9660685-1-3
        1. Baldwin, Richard L.   2. Pianists—United
        States—Biography. I. Title.
ML417.B35 A3   1999
786.2' .092   [B]dc—21   CIP

PROJECT COORDINATION BY JENKINS GROUP, INC.

03 02 01 00 ♦ 5 4 3 2 1

Printed in the United States of America

This true story is dedicated to my mother, Margaret McMillan Baldwin who gave her gift of music to her family and all who listened. Playing the piano was her God-given talent. "Mom, would you play…" or "Marg, please play…" were entrees into a joyful musical experience.

Acknowledgments

I wish to thank my editor Holly Sasso, for her suggestions and guidance in effectively telling this story. I thank my illustrator Jan Kenny who so accurately captured the spirit behind this story. I thank Mrs. Henes for her skill in teaching children with and without disabilities and for welcoming me into the wonderful world of creating music, a medium enjoyed by all and a unifying force that can bring us together. Finally, I thank the boys and girls who accepted me and taught me a marvelous lesson. It is often said that when a lesson needs to be learned, the teacher will appear.

Introduction

*T*his is a story of acceptance. If this story could be universally experienced, it would bring peace and joy to all. What you are about to read really happened, and it can happen over and over in our hearts, minds and souls. It is a story of hope, a story of accepting others.

The Piano Recital

When he was fifty years old, he decided to resume the piano lessons he had taken as a young boy. He wanted to bring back some of the magic he remembered, listening to his mother effortlessly move her fingers across the keyboard without looking at a single note.

Mrs. Henes was willing to teach adults. She had patience and understood his hectic life which did not allow practicing lessons to be a priority. He took his lessons, learned theory, and was able, with some practice and good teaching, to play familiar music.

One day, Mrs. Henes said, "I would like you to consider playing in the June recital." His response was quick and clear. "I don't do recitals." At 51 years of age, he decided he did not need the experience of performing his weekly practiced piano lessons among a talented group of youngsters and their parents. He would stand out as a grandfather to some and a father to all.

What hair he had was gray. In addition, he had a hearing loss since infancy and has worn two hearing aids which bring attention to the fact that he has a disability. He was quite certain to be out of place, not only physically in comparison to children, but also in musical talent, or the lack of it!

As he thought more about the recital, he realized that a piano recital naturally goes with piano lessons. All the other students were busy preparing for the recital, and he slowly realized that he should be too. If the recital audience had a problem with a 51-year-old, bald man with a hearing impairment on the program with children, then the audience had the problem. He was where he was, a late bloomer. He decided to play in the recital.

Weeks went by. With each lesson, he fine-tuned the pieces that were to be performed. At the dress rehearsal, the students lined up in the order of their skill, which placed him fifth out of seventeen. He was in front of Jason, a thirteen-year-old with a good head on his shoulders. Jason's weekly lesson was after his and he was a familiar face. The only other student he knew was Justin, an eight-year-old young man. Justin preceded him at his weekly lesson so he too was familiar. He didn't know the other fourteen boys and girls; the dress rehearsal was the first time he had seen any of them.

The next day, he had his last weekly lesson. Mrs. Henes suggested that he might feel more comfortable if he did not line up with the children but that he walk in with her, sit with her, and go to the piano when it was his time to play. He trusted her perceptions.

Before he knew it, the day of the recital was upon him. He had agreed to meet his wife, Patty, at a restaurant close to the church where the recital was to be held. He found that he wasn't hungry. His body and mind were nervous anticipating the performance. "I wish Mom was living to hear me play," said the man. Patty replied, "I think she will be there, enjoying every moment."

Picking at his tossed salad, he finally blurted out, "I don't know why I agreed to do this." Patty replied, "I don't know why you did either!" His earlier thoughts came back. Why would a 51-year-old man, just beginning to learn to play the piano and being so out-of-place with a group of talented children, subject himself to a public performance? He had enough stress in his life without willfully adding another challenging experience, especially when he would stick out like a sore thumb! But, his name was on the program, the decision had been made, and the recital was to be performed.

He drove to the church thinking, "At least I am the only participant who can drive to this event." Inside the church he saw Jason, Justin, and the other children.

He said to Jason, "Man, I am nervous."

"Aw you'll do OK," Jason replied. "If you get stuck, just stop, get yourself together, and go on."

"Thanks," he said. Jason seemed confident and he appreciated his advice. After all, he was an old pro. This was Jason's fifth recital.

About 10 minutes before their processional into the church they were all asked to gather in the pastor's office. Mrs. Henes gave them some last-minute instructions and then asked them to hold hands as she offered a prayer. They stood in a circle and listened as she thanked God for their talent and their opportunity to share it with others. She asked for His divine guidance in their performances and asked Him to bless their families who offered support for their playing. She then told them to relax and instructed them to get into line while she went out into the church to check on final details.

The children scurried into position as they had lined up in their dress rehearsal. The man stayed in the back as suggested by his teacher. Jason noticed that he was not in front of him, but was away from the group. Jason got the man's attention, and with the children watching, motioned for him to get in line and take his position in front of him.

The man responded loud enough for all to hear, "Mrs. Henes told me to stay back, walk in with her, and sit with her."

Jason thought for a moment and then, shaking his head back and forth, motioned once again for the man to come up and get in the line. In the few seconds that the man hesitated, a couple of the children came up, and taking his arms, brought him to his position in the line, right in front of Jason. Mrs. Henes walked back through the door to find all of the recital partici-

The Piano Recital

pants ready to go with the man in the fifth position. He sheepishly told her that the children thought he should be in the line with them.

"Where do you want to be?" she asked.

"I think I want to be here," he said. She smiled and nodded, and in a matter of seconds, the door opened and they paraded in front of their audience.

Just before it was his turn to get up and go to the piano, he felt a soft touch on his arm. He looked to his left and heard

Jason say very sincerely and reassuredly, "Good luck." The man nodded and walked up to the piano. He began, and while his heart beat faster than he thought possible, with only

The Piano Recital

a mistake or two, he managed to play both pieces. He took his rehearsed bow to polite and friendly applause. He returned to his seat and became relaxed enough to appreciate the wonderful gift of music that each of his fellow students possessed.

After the recital, Patty came by to give him a hug and he knew she was proud of him. One of the mothers said, "You are an inspiration and a role model for my son."

One man shook his hand and said, "Boy, that takes a lot of guts to get up there with those kids!"

"Yes, it sure does," the man replied. "I didn't think my heart could beat that fast."

Jason's mother came by and introduced herself. The man told her about Jason's kindness and maturity - and his very meaningful "Good luck" comment.

It was not until after this experience that the man realized the lesson that he had been given: We live in a society where the standard of acceptance seems to revolve around fitting into people's preconceived ideas of what is normal. We find ourselves excluding, or wanting to be separated from, people for a number of reasons - because of their ideas, dress, looks, economic status, political views, disability, nationality, behavior, or state of health. What we should desire is to celebrate diversity and to value our differences. We should free ourselves from judging others and commit to giving all our unconditional love.

What runs through his mind now is that each of his young classmates was an inspiration and a model for him! What he experienced was acceptance. Here he was, a man 51 years of age, unknown to most of the children, bald, wearing hearing aids and what was said by their actions was, "You are one of us.

You are a piano player. You belong." And he, like many who fall into subgroups, felt like saying, "But I am not like you. I am older, I am bald, I am hearing impaired, I am not fitting into your preconceived image of a recital participant." Luckily, that is not what happened. They shared music. Together they shared acceptance; they valued and appreciated their differences.

All of this happened without a lecture on accepting others, without discussion, without pamphlets and books. It happened as a reminder that we can come together, and that people can be encouraged to join the human line no matter what differences we possess that make us unique and special. Just as Jason and the others would not accept his being outside the line of piano players, we must not accept people being outside of the line of humans in general. We all share this planet where each has a part to play in the recital called life.

Epilogue

This story really happened to me, for I was that 51-year-old, bald, hearing impaired man who was accepted by the children. I thought I was receiving a piano lesson but what I received was a lesson in living. Isn't life like that? We often get something very different from what we expect.

I'm often asked, when I finish telling this story, if I still play the piano. The answer is "No." I took lessons for another year, played in a second recital at a nursing home, and then found myself having more fun writing stories. This passion soon became the reason to form a publishing company so that my stories could be shared with others.

Oh, and one more thing. I found that I didn't have to play the piano to feel the presence of my mother. She is in every song I hear or sing and she lives every time I tell, or you read this story.

Thank you for reading my story. May we, as Jason did for me, bring all people into the human line. We are all connected. We are each other, sharing this earthly experience.

About Mrs. Henes: Mrs. Christine Henes is a music therapist who now lives in Cottage Grove, Wisconsin. She still gives piano lessons and works her magic in so many ways.

About the Illustrator: Jan Kenny lives in Manistee, Michigan, and enjoys drawing. She specializes in a Victorian motif and is admired by many for her talent.

About the Author: Richard L. Baldwin wrote this story in 1994 when he was Michigan's Director of Special Education. He was so moved by the experience that he often told what he called, "The Piano Story" at conferences and wherever people would enjoy the lesson he had learned. Some people heard it often and many would ask him to tell his "Piano Story." Because there was such an interest in this story, Rich decided to write it so that many could enjoy it. Rich lives with his wife, Patty, in Haslett, Michigan.

If you wish to correspond with Rich you may write to him c/o Buttonwood Press, P.O. Box 716, Haslett, Michigan 48840. His e-mail address is RLBald@aol.com You are invited to visit the website of Buttonwood Press at www.buttonwoodpress.com

To order an additional copy of
The Piano Recital

Michigan Residents: A copy of *The Piano Recital* costs $9.95 (includes Michigan sales tax and shipping and handling).

Non-Michigan Residents: A copy of *The Piano Recital* costs $9.50 (includes shipping and handling).

A check made payable to **Buttonwood Press** and ordering information should be mailed to:

Buttonwood Press
P. O. Box 716
Haslett, MI 48840

PLEASE PRINT

Name: _____

Address: _____

City: _____

State: _____ Zip: _____

For multiple orders please contact Buttonwood Press via fax at (517) 339-5908 or via e-mail, RLBald@aol.com or via address: P.O. Box 716, Haslett, Michigan 48840.

Be sure to visit our website at www.buttonwoodpress.com for information about books written by Richard L. Baldwin.

Thank you!